SCALE HIGH™
School, Career, and Life Enrichment

SCALE High Student Workbook

Grade 9-12

Created by Dupé Aleru

Printed in the United States of America

First Edition, 2017

ISBN 978-0-9993214-1-6

Cover Design and Illustrations by Alex M. Smith

www.scalehigh.org

Table of Contents

Welcome Letter

Dear Student,

On behalf of Tutors for Tots, Tweens & Teens LLC, I am pleased to welcome you to the SCALE High Program. We are delighted to work with you during this exciting time of your life. As you read through this Student Workbook, you will be introduced to the many benefits of SCALE High that will help you identify, define, and achieve your future goals.

The SCALE High Program connects students who aspire to achieve a high level of success in all aspects of their lives with mentors who can help them achieve these goals. Goal-setting is encouraged and expected from all student participants. Active participation and continued motivation throughout the 8-week program are essential for student success. This is the time where you should be thinking about your gifts and talents. What are you good at? What type of person do you want to become? Over the next eight weeks, you will be able to answer these questions. Our program model is designed to help you set SMART goals that prepare you for the journey ahead.

Your coach is here to guide, support, and challenge you during this important time of your life. The value of the benefits derived from the SCALE High Program entirely depends on your attitude during the program, performance, and dedication towards your academic success. What you put in will determine what you get out. Take initiative to engage with your academic coach and make use of the endless opportunities that present themselves during the program. Have a positive attitude, participate in all the weekly exercises, and don't forget to have fun. I wish you the best of luck in all your future endeavors.

Warmest wishes,

Dupé Eplery

Founder and Owner
SCALE High Program

Duties and Program Rules

Student Expectations

- Have a positive attitude
- Have a willingness to learn and succeed
- Be open and honest with your Coach
- Be respectful of your Coach at all times
- Use appropriate language during school and program hours
- Leave all electronics in a backpack or purse during the program
- Adhere to school rules, policies, and procedures at all times
- Come to sessions on time and ready to learn
- Bring all necessary materials to the sessions
- Stay organized with the given materials
- Participate in all individual or group exercises
- Listen to your Coach

Program Rules

Come to the sessions prepared

Be respectful

Listen to instructions

No cellphones

No sidebar conversations

Participate in all exercises

Introduction

About SCALE High
SCALE High brings together skilled college students and teachers to mentor high school students in the area of goal-setting. The program empowers the high school students to embrace a positive way of thinking that will inspire them to *scale high* when planning for the future.

Our Mission
It is the mission of SCALE High to provide high school students with the knowledge of how to set SMART goals in every aspect of their lives while mastering the art of taking action. As a result, students will be better equipped to think about the future and be motivated to turn their visions into reality.

What Does SCALE High Stand For?
SCALE stands for School, Career, and Life Enrichment.

Why Set Goals?
People in all walks of life—from athletes to entrepreneurs—set goals in order to be successful. Setting goals will help students choose where they want to go in life. And by knowing exactly what they want to accomplish, students will learn where they have to start.

Expected Student Outcomes
By the end of the 8-week program, each student who has successfully completed the SCALE High curriculum will know and understand how to:
- Set SMART goals
- Be well prepared in all academic disciplines
- Have a higher motivation to succeed in all endeavors they set out to do
- Exhibit a sense of pride and satisfaction in their performance

8-Week Lesson Plan

For each week you will complete two exercises. You should meet with your Coach twice a week for 30-45 minutes.	**Lessons and Exercises**	**SCALE Board**
Week 1	• Meet & Greet • Intro to SCALE High • Questionnaire • Exercise 1	Cut out 3 pictures and keep in folder
Week 2	• School Credit • Exercise 2 • Attendance • Exercise 3	Cut out 3 pictures and keep in folder
Week 3	• Organization • Exercise 4 • Time Management • Exercise 5	Cut out 3 pictures and keep in folder
Week 4	• Career Options • Exercise 6 • Career Search • Exercise 7	Cut out 3 pictures and keep in folder
Week 5	• Application Process • Exercise 8 • Mock Interview • Exercise 9	Cut out 3 pictures and keep in folder
Week 6	• Paths to College • Exercise 10 • Financial Aid • Exercise 11	Cut out 3 pictures and keep in folder
Week 7	• School Mirrors Work • Exercise 12 • Recap • Exercise 13	Cut out 3 pictures and keep in folder
Week 8	• SCALE Board • Exercise 14 • Exit Survey (administered by Coach)	Put your SCALE board together. Share with Coach and classmates.

School

Set the Foundation

1-2 Year Goals

Week 1

Exercise 1

Exercise 1

Name: Date:

Student Directions: Go over the questionnaire with your Coach and explain why you answered each question the way you did. Then fill out the below flow chart by listing six School goals. Write your answers – as bullet points – in the blue boxes. Be as specific as possible.

Once you have completed this chart, keep it in a safe place, as you will be using it later in the program.

Examples:
School goal – have perfect attendance for the rest of the semester
Career goal – get accepted into a CSU
Life goal – have a family one day

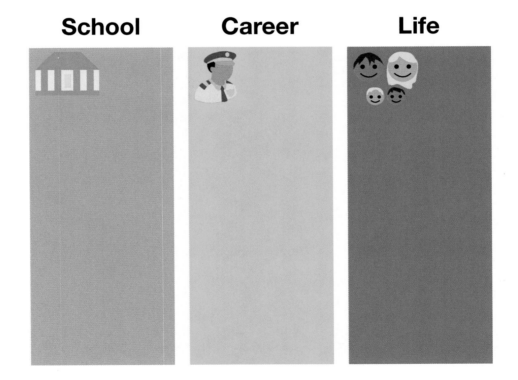

Week 2

Exercise 2
and
Exercise 3

Credit Planner

Student Directions: After reviewing your transcripts, enter the total number of credits needed for each subject in the left column. Also enter the completed credits per subject and quarter.

Credits Needed	Subject	Ninth Fall	Ninth Spring	Tenth Fall	Tenth Spring	Eleventh Fall	Eleventh Spring	Twelfth Fall	Twelfth Spring
_____	History Social Science 3 years								
_____	English 3 years								
_____	Mathematics 2 years								
_____	Science or Integrated Science 2 years								
_____	Language or Fine Arts 1 year								
_____	Physical Education 2 years								
_____	Electives								
___/___	Total Credits								

Check if applicable: ▢ Algebra 1 passed

Weekly Class Attendance Record

Name: Date:

Student Directions: Circle one of the following for your class each week.

Class_____ Teacher_____ Room#_____

T = Tardy   U = Unexcused Absence   E = Excused Absence   P = Present

Week 1	Monday				Tuesday				Wednesday				Thursday				Friday			
	T	U	E	P	T	U	E	P	T	U	E	P	T	U	E	P	T	U	E	P
Week 2	Monday				Tuesday				Wednesday				Thursday				Friday			
	T	U	E	P	T	U	E	P	T	U	E	P	T	U	E	P	T	U	E	P
Week 3	Monday				Tuesday				Wednesday				Thursday				Friday			
	T	U	E	P	T	U	E	P	T	U	E	P	T	U	E	P	T	U	E	P
Week 4	Monday				Tuesday				Wednesday				Thursday				Friday			
	T	U	E	P	T	U	E	P	T	U	E	P	T	U	E	P	T	U	E	P
Week 5	Monday				Tuesday				Wednesday				Thursday				Friday			
	T	U	E	P	T	U	E	P	T	U	E	P	T	U	E	P	T	U	E	P
Week 6	Monday				Tuesday				Wednesday				Thursday				Friday			
	T	U	E	P	T	U	E	P	T	U	E	P	T	U	E	P	T	U	E	P
Week 7	Monday				Tuesday				Wednesday				Thursday				Friday			
	T	U	E	P	T	U	E	P	T	U	E	P	T	U	E	P	T	U	E	P
Week 8	Monday				Tuesday				Wednesday				Thursday				Friday			
	T	U	E	P	T	U	E	P	T	U	E	P	T	U	E	P	T	U	E	P

Exercise 4
and
Exercise 5

Student Organization Checklist

Name: Date:

Student Directions: Go through your binder and check off every item that you have that is shown below. If you are missing any item from what you see below, make a list and a note to purchase these items so that you can be more efficient and organized in school.

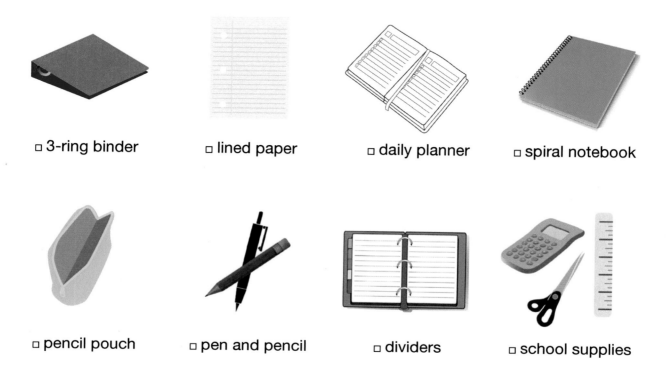

□ 3-ring binder   □ lined paper   □ daily planner   □ spiral notebook

□ pencil pouch   □ pen and pencil   □ dividers   □ school supplies

DON'T FORGET: Purchase a sturdy 3-ring binder that will last you the entire year. Be sure to place tabbed or color-coded dividers to separate your classes. Use pocket dividers to separate classwork, completed homework, and exams.

Keeping a daily planner will allow you to keep your homework assignments organized by due date, know when to study for an exam, and remember school events. Loose-leaf paper allows for easy use and access, while a spiral notebook can be used to take class notes. Decide what needs to stay in your binder and keep all other supplies in a supply box or pouch.

How Well I Manage My Time

Name: Date:

Student Directions: How well do you manage your time when you need to study? Answer the following questions and use the scoring guide below to calculate your final score.

Agree = 3 points   Sometimes = 2 points   Disagree = 1 point

Affirmation	Points
I have successfully prepared a quiet place to study that has limited distractions.	
I have established a set schedule for the time that I will study every day after school.	
I have all my materials within reach in my study environment so I do not have to get up.	
I write my homework assignments in my daily planner or notebook, and check it regularly.	
I ask a knowledgeable person for help if I do not understand my assignment or homework.	
I do not wait until the last minute to study for exams, as I know it will not be beneficial to my success.	
I am responsible for bringing my textbooks home so I can successfully complete my homework.	
I have a binder with dividers so I can organize the materials for each of my classes, by period.	

Total Points   _____

Check out your score!

If you scored:

18-24	**Five stars!** You have outstanding study skills. Keep up the great work!
9-17	**So-So:** You have some good habits, but you can learn more.
8	**Uh-Oh:** You could use some help with your study habits. Discuss with your Coach.

Time Management Study Plan

Name: Date:

Student Directions: Complete the exercise below. This is your opportunity to make a plan to better organize yourself and your time.

I have a quiet place to study.   My quiet place at home will be *(indicate place):*
□ Yes   □ No

_____

I have my study place set up.   My study place will be set up by *(indicate date):*
□ Yes   □ No

_____

The most practical time of day for me to study is *(check one):*
□ Morning   □ Afternoon   □ Evening   □ Night

I play sports or participate in extracurricular activities that cause my schedule to vary from day to day:
□ Yes, it varies   □ It rarely varies   □ It does not vary

My study routine will be as follows *(indicate times):*

Mondays from _____ to _____

Tuesdays from _____ to _____

Wednesdays from _____ to _____

Thursdays from _____ to _____

Fridays from _____ to _____

I will begin implementing my study routine on *(indicate date):*
_____

I, _____ as a participant in the SCALE High Program, promise to adhere to my time management study plan throughout the school year in order to improve my organizational skills and study habits.

Career

Build

5-year Goals

Level 2

Week 4

Exercise 6
and
Exercise 7

My Dream Career

Student Directions: List three activities you enjoy doing and state why you enjoy doing them. Then list three possible careers you would be interested in pursuing.

List three activities that you enjoy doing and never get tired of doing:

I enjoy _____

because _____

I enjoy _____

because _____

I enjoy _____

because _____

List your top three possible career choices and explain why you like them:

1) _____

_____

_____

2) _____

_____

_____

3) _____

_____

_____

My Job and Career Search

Name: Date:

Student Directions: You will use the CalJobs site to seek potential job or career choices. Type www.caljobs.ca.gov in your web browser and follow the steps below.

Write down your answers for one (1) job search and keep it in your folder, to be used later. Repeat the steps below for two other searches.

Note: The layout of the website may change over time.

- **Home Page:** on the left side of the webpage, click *"Find a Job."*

- **Quick Job Search:** in the *"Search Criteria"* box, enter a keyword that describes the career title you are interested in (e.g., police officer), then click "Search."

- **Summary:** you will be shown a summary of jobs in your area. Each summary will list: Job Title / Description Snippet; Employer; Location; and Salary. Click on the "Detailed" tab to the right of "Results View" (at the top) to read additional details of each position.

- **Job Details:** scroll down to view the list of jobs, then click on any of the highlighted job titles to view additional information.

- **Job Summary/Job Description:** scroll down the page to view and read the following:

  a)   Job Title
  b)   Employer Name
  c)   City, State, Zip
  d)   Date the Job Posted
  e)   Positions Available
  f)   Occupation
  g)   Job Requirements
  h)   Job Properties
  i)   Salary
  j)   Job Description
  k)   Additional Information

- Click the "Home" button in the upper left corner, and repeat the steps for two more keywords.

Exercise 8
and
Exercise 9

Sample Resume

John Doe
10 Highland Avenue
Long Beach, CA 90804
(555) 555-5555
john.doe@myemail.com

Education   Highland Park High School, class of 2017 (3.9 GPA)

Experience
Long Beach Grill—Busboy (August 2016 - present)
- Cleaned tabletops and ensured that fresh tablecloths and mats are placed
- Provided waiters or waitresses with information of new customer arrival
- Organized and cleaned dishes in the kitchen and expedited orders
- Assisted customers looking for service

National Honor Society—Volunteer Assistant (2015 - present)
Participated in numerous volunteer activities, including:
- Building a house for Habitat for Humanity (30 hours)
- Collecting food for Meals on Wheels (50 hours)
- Organizing events for the National Honor Society

Activities
- Chess Club (4 years)—participated in state and national tournaments
- Yearbook Club (3 years)—coordinated layout and content

Skills
- Strong interpersonal skills, oral, and written communication skills
- Customer service skills
- Ability to work as part of a team and follow instructions
- Ability to incorporate technology (Microsoft Office, social media)

References
Available upon request

Contact Information: place this at the top of your resume, in the center with bold font. Include: name, address, phone number, and email.

Education: include school, graduation date, and GPA (if it is 3.0 or higher).

Experience: include title and dates followed by a bulleted or narrative list. Begin each bullet with an active verb (e.g., coordinated, organized, participated).

Activities: list your academic, school, and extracurricular activities.

Skills: a good way to find the skills you need for the job is to check the job requirements in the job positing. Otherwise, use the general skills that you possess.

Sample Cover Letter

John Doe
10 Highland Avenue
Long Beach, CA 90804
(555) 555-5555
john.doe@myemail.com

1

April 15, 2017

2

Ms. Dupé R. Aleru
5541 E. 7th Street
Long Beach, CA 90804

3

Dear Ms. Aleru,

4

I am applying for the in-home tutoring position as advertised on BeachLink, via California State University, Long Beach website. I have experience tutoring in mathematics and I think I would be a great addition to your tutoring organization.

5

I was a peer tutor at my former high school for four years, tutoring Algebra I through Calculus III. In all my mathematics courses—including the AP courses—I received a B letter grade or higher.

My desire is to be able to add value to Tutors for Tots. I admire how your organization has been helping students achieve academic success since 2010.

I hope that you will consider me for the position. You may contact me by phone (555) 555-5555 or by email john.doe@myemail.com.

I look forward to speaking with you to discuss my experience and how I can be of benefit to Tutors for Tots, Tweens & Teens LLC.

Sincerely,

6

John Doe

7

1 **Contact Information:** the first section or header should include your: name, address, phone number (or cellphone number), and email address.

2 **Date:** use the current date that you are sending the email, fax, or letter.

3 **Return Address:** do your research to find the return address of the employer.

4 **Salutation:** find out the name of the individual you're sending the letter. Try to avoid, "To Whom It May Concern" as it may look unprofessional; like you didn't put in the effort.

5 **Body:** 1st paragraph: why you are writing; 2nd paragraph: what you have to offer the employer; 3rd paragraph: your knowledge of the company; 4th paragraph: your closing.

6 **Closing:** complimentary closing.

7 **Signature:** type your name then sign your name (scanned or an image).

Mock Interview

Before the Interview

- **Research the company** – know as much as possible about the company, including the interviewer's name, before you walk through the doors.
- **Ask questions** – asking questions and participating during the interview gives the impression that you are interested, so be sure to make your list beforehand.
- **Mock interview** – practice a mock interview with an adult. Be sure to make eye contact and give clear answers to any questions asked.
- **Anticipate questions** – go over potential interview questions that the interviewer may ask you (e.g., your strengths and weaknesses).

Day of the Interview

- **Dress to impress** – showing up formally dressed or in business casual is always best. Be sure to iron your clothes and look presentable.
- **Be punctual** – an old saying goes, "If you're on time, you're late." Be sure to arrive 10-15 minutes before your scheduled interview time.
- **Bring materials** – always have on hand an extra copy of your resume and cover letter, in addition to references, letters of recommendation, and any certifications that might be beneficial to the position to which you are applying.

During the Interview

- **Be courteous** – greet everyone at the location and use good manners.
- **Be personable** – show off your personality, but keep greetings short and simple.

After the Interview

- **Thank your interviewer** – shake hands with the interviewer and later send a thank you card or email; and follow up in two weeks.

Exercise 10
and
Exercise 11

Paths to College Quiz

Name: Date:

1. Can you obtain a Ph.D. at a California State University (CSU)?   □ Yes □ No

2. Do most Community Colleges require you to take the SAT or ACT?   □ Yes □ No

3. What is the highest level of education a person can obtain?
□   Associate degree (A.A.)
□   High school diploma
□   Master's degree (M.A., M.S., M.F.A.)
□   Doctoral or professional degree (Ph.D., J.D., M.D.)
□   Bachelor's degree (B.A., B.S.)

4. The following are either part of a 2-year college or 4-year university system. Check the one that does not apply:
□   University of California
□   California State University
□   Vocational College
□   Magnet School
□   Career College

5. The A-G requirements are classes you must take and pass in order to:
□   Graduate from high school
□   Get into graduate school
□   Get accepted to a University of California (UC) or California State University (CSU)
□   Take the SAT or ACT
□   Gain acceptance into a trade school

Financial Aid Crossword Puzzle

Student Directions: Fill out the crossword puzzle using the clues below. If you need assistance, refer back to your manual that defined the four types of financial aid.

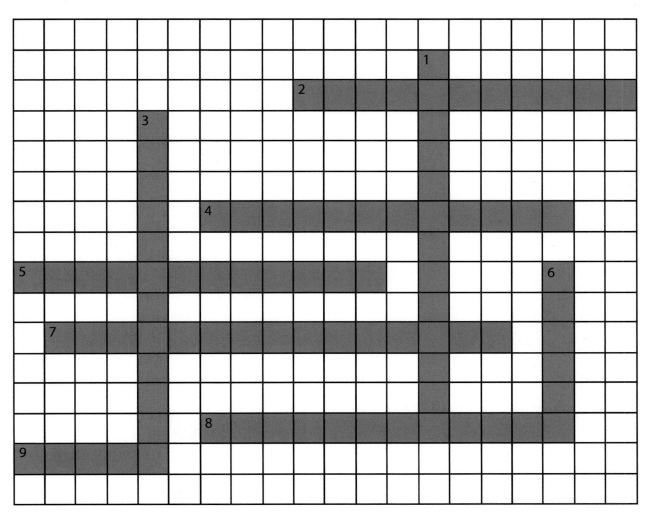

Word Bank

☐ private loans   ☐ scholarships   ☐ grants   ☐ loans   ☐ federal grants
☐ employment loans   ☐ state grants   ☐ financial aid   ☐ federal loans

Across	Down
2 For state residents only	1 Based on your financial needs
4 Helps students meet their college expenses	3 Loans you must pay back
5 Credit-based loans that help bridge the gap	6 Federal and state types offered
7 A federal work-study that's federally funded	
8 Private money that you don't have to pay back	
9 Federal and private types offered	

Level 3

Life

BIG Picture

10-year Goals

Exercise 12
and
Exercise 13

School Mirrors the Workplace

Name: Date:

Student Directions: School mirrors the workplace in many ways. See if you can figure out the similarities and discuss them with your Coach. Identify the similarities by placing the *letters* in the left column on the correct *lines* in the right column.

School	**Workplace**
a. Principal	_____ Coworkers
b. School Rules	_____ Job Applications
c. Peers	_____ Employee
d. Attendance Records	_____ Workplace
e. College Applications	_____ Policies & Procedure
f. Student	_____ Resume
g. Cumulative Files	_____ Employer
h. Classroom	_____ Time Sheets

My SCALE High Experience

Name: _____   Date: _____

Student Directions: Take a few moments to think about your SCALE High experience and consider how the program has impacted your life—we hope it did. Do you feel more motivated? Have you made plans to speak with a counselor about your credits, graduation, or career options? Use the space below to talk about your experience and your future goal-setting plans.

Things I did not know, but I am now informed about are: _____

_____

_____

_____

My favorite part of the program was: _____

_____

_____

_____

The goals that I will get started on right away are: _____

_____

_____

_____

An "Ah-Ha" moment I had was when: _____

_____

_____

_____

_____

One important thing I will take away from this program is: _____

_____

Exercise 14

Steps to Achieve My Goals

Name: Date:

Student Directions: Choose *two* goals from each tier in "Exercise 1." Use the space below to write down the steps you need to take to achieve these goals.

Steps needed to achieve my 1-2 year goals:

- _____
  _____
  _____

- _____
  _____
  _____

Steps needed to achieve my 5-year goals:

- _____
  _____
  _____

- _____
  _____
  _____

Steps needed to achieve my 10-year goals:

- _____
  _____
  _____

- _____
  _____
  _____

In Closing

The SCALE High Program was specifically designed to inspire high school students like yourself as you develop a roadmap that will help you become successful in all walks of life. The purpose of the 8-week program is to have you explore what you desire to achieve from school, a career, and life. By completing this program, you will start to envision what you want to accomplish in these three areas, and take action to achieve your goals.

Congratulations on your achievement and dedication to completing the program. Best of luck in everything you set out to do. Use the tools and skills that you learned in this program to reach new heights. As you go through life, keep your SCALE board as a reminder to *scale high* and continue on your journey towards living the life you are meant to live.

Goals

1. Land a kickflip.
2. Get straight A's.
3. Introduce myself to someone new.
4. Believe in myself.
5. Think about my future.

Handouts

College Systems Handout

Take these steps to prepare for acceptance at a University of California (UC)
- Fulfill the A-G requirement by the end of high school
- Graduate and receive your diploma from high school
- Earn as many A's and B's as possible
- Have a minimum 3.0 GPA
- Take the PSAT your sophomore year of high school
- Take the SAT or ACT your junior year, and once again by the end of your senior year (take either or both the SAT/ACT)
- To assist in paying for college, apply for financial aid before the deadline

Take these steps to prepare for acceptance at a California State University (CSU)
- Fulfill the A-G requirement by the end of high school
- Graduate and receive your diploma from high school
- Earn as many A's and B's as possible
- Have a minimum 2.0 GPA
- Take the PSAT your sophomore year of high school
- Take the SAT or ACT your junior year, and once again by the end of your senior year (take either or both the SAT/ACT)
- To assist in paying for college, apply for financial aid before the deadline

Take these steps to prepare for acceptance at a Community College/Junior College (JC)
- Take some A-G courses during high school
- Graduate and receive your diploma from high school
- Earn as many A's and B's as possible
- Contact each college you want to attend to find out its minimum GPA requirement
- Take the PSAT your sophomore year of high school
- Take the SAT or ACT – it will not hurt to have it on your records (take either or both the SAT/ACT)
- To assist in paying for college, apply for financial aid before the deadline

A-G Requirement Handout

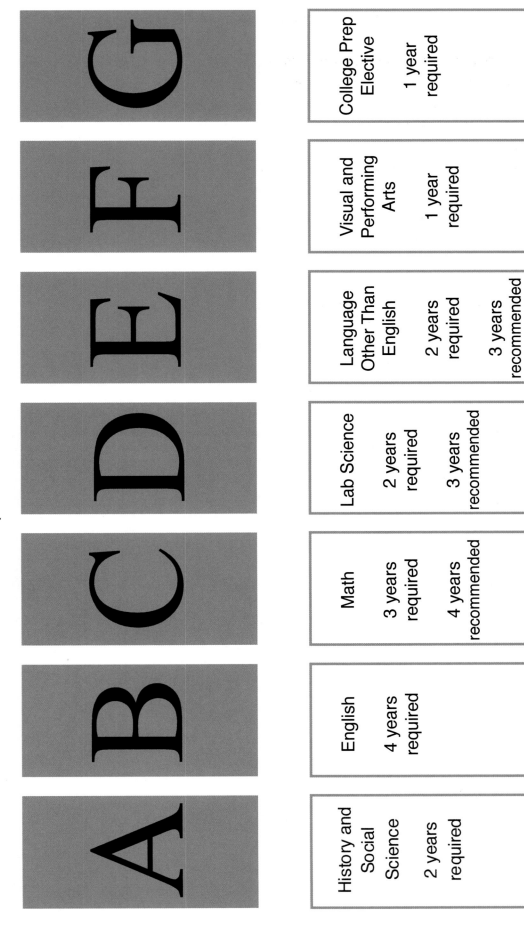

Letter	Subject	Requirement
A	History and Social Science	2 years required
B	English	4 years required
C	Math	3 years required / 4 years recommended
D	Lab Science	2 years required / 3 years recommended
E	Language Other Than English	2 years required / 3 years recommended
F	Visual and Performing Arts	1 year required
G	College Prep Elective	1 year required

Financial Aid & Grants Handout

There are **FOUR** types of financial aid: ***scholarships, grants, loans,*** and ***employment.***

Scholarships: Scholarships are private money given to students from community groups, donors, or the university. The great thing about scholarships is that you do not have to pay them back.

Federal grants: There are four types of federal student aid grants, one specialized grant, and loan combo. All grants are awarded based on the information you submit to FASFA. FASFA bases the grants on financial need by calculating your expected family contribution (EFC).

State grants: These grants are for California state residents only (or your state, if you're outside of California). Your residency status is usually determined by your university's Office of Admission at the time of your application.

Federal loans: These are loans from the federal government. You must pay back the funds given to you.

Private loans: Private lenders give you these loans based on your credit. These loans help bridge the gap between the actual cost of your tuition, your other financial aid funds, and the amount you will contribute.

Employment: This federal work study offers employment opportunities to students and is federally funded. The program usually has limited space. However, if given the opportunity, you can benefit from this program. Work study is also given to students with the highest financial need.

SCALE High's goal-setting curriculum is designed for high school students to reflect—examine and interpret—upon their life experiences and transform their deepest passions into reality. This reflection process allows students to become more self-aware and discover how their gifts and talents can be of service to the world.

SCALE High hopes to partner with high schools (public or private); districts; county offices of education; group homes; and other educational institutions, community organizations, and businesses.

Dupé Aleru

Founder and Owner of Tutors for Tots, Tweens & Teens LLC

Acknowledgements

Many thanks to Mr. Saldana—the former Principal at Beach High School in Long Beach, CA—who was the first person to give us the opportunity to implement our program. Also, a special thanks to Abigail Aparicio, who kindly volunteered to help launch the SCALE High Program during the Fall of 2014. Last but not least, thank you to the teachers, who have always been an inspiration to this work.

About the Founder

Dupé Aleru is an entrepreneur, curriculum developer, business coach, and motivational speaker.

As an alumna of California State University, Long Beach, Dupé obtained a B.A. in Sociology and a Multiple Subject Teaching Credential. She also holds a M.S. in Educational Counseling and a Pupil Personnel Services Credential from the University of La Verne.

After four years of teaching for Long Beach Unified School District, Dupé took a job as the Director of Education Services for *The Beverly Hills Courier,* where she built the education section of the newspaper from the ground up, in less than one year.

In 2010, she founded Tutors for Tots, Tweens & Teens LLC—one of Southern California's elite educational companies for students PK-12. Her body of work includes, "The Cook Book" 12-episode web series, its spin-off program "The Cook Book Nutrition Course," the SCALE High Program, and a children's book titled *Animals in Action A-Z.*

Dupé Aleru

Tutors for Tots, Tweens & Teens LLC

5541 E. 7th Street

Long Beach, CA 90804

(562) 856-2801

www.tutorsfortots.com

info@tutorfortots.com

SCALE High Program

www.scalehigh.org

scalehigh@scalehigh.org

Real Teachers. Better Results. ™

Made in the USA
Lexington, KY
27 May 2019